# Colour

## Macdonald

## About Macdonald Starters

Macdonald Starters are vocabulary controlled information books for young children. More than ninety per cent of the words in the text will be in the reading vocabulary of the vast majority of young readers. Word and sentence length have also been carefully controlled.

Key new words associated with the topic of each book are repeated with picture explanations in the Starters dictionary at the end. The dictionary can also be used as an index for teaching children to look things up.

Teachers and experts have been consulted on the content and accuracy of the books.

A MACDONALD BOOK

© Macdonald & Co (Publishers) Ltd 1971

First published in
Great Britain in 1971

This edition first published in
Great Britain in 1986

British Library Cataloguing in Publication Data
Colour. – (Starters)
    1. Readers – 1950 –
    I. Title
    428.6    PE1119
    ISBN 0-356-03962 -5
    ISBN 0-356-11488-0 Pbk

Printed and bound in Great Britain by
Purnell & Sons (Book Production) Ltd,
Paulton, Bristol

Published by Macdonald & Co (Publishers) Ltd
Maxwell House
74 Worship Street
London EC2A 2EN

Members of BPCC plc

Illustrators: Ann Ricketts, Michael Ricketts

This is our school.
We are painting.
We are using
different coloured paints.

1

I am painting a dragon.
I am mixing blue and red.
It makes purple.
His tail is purple.

2

When I mix blue and yellow
it makes green.
Red and yellow make orange.
The dragon breathes orange fire.

These men are doing a war dance.
They have painted their bodies.
The paint is called war paint.

These are people who live in India.
They are acting in an Indian play.
Their faces are painted
in lots of colours.

People use colours to say things.
Sometimes red means DANGER.

6

Traffic lights use colours.
Red means STOP.
Green means GO.

These berries are
brightly coloured.
This helps the birds to see them.

Male birds
are often brightly coloured.
The female birds
are a different colour.

European hornet

honeybee

bumblebee

digger wasp

wasp

blister beetle

Insects which can hurt
are often black and yellow.
10

Other insects use colour
to help them hide.
This insect is green.
It looks like a green leaf.

Large animals often use their colour.
Lions can hide in yellow grass.

12

These animals are chameleons.
They can change colour.
This helps them hide.

These soldiers are wearing green.
Other people cannot see them
among the trees.

14

This man lived long ago in Rome.
He had a purple band
on his clothes.
This showed he was important.

15

These footballers wear red.
This shows which team
they play for.
The other team wear blue.

This ship is flying many flags.
Different coloured flags
are used to send messages.

Cloth is coloured with dye.
Dye is like paint for cloth.
Some cloth is dyed in plain colours.
Some cloth is dyed in patterns.
18

Pictures in books
are coloured like this.
There are a lot of little dots.
The dots are made with coloured ink.

19

Rays of sunlight
are shining through this water.
You can see colours
in the sunlight.

20

This is a rainbow.
Sunlight is shining through the rain.
It makes colours.

## See for yourself

You can make pictures
using paint and corks.
Have one cork
for each colour paint.

22

# Starter's **Colour** words

**school**
(page 1)

**purple**
(page 2)

**paint**
(page 1)

**yellow**
(page 3)

**dragon**
(page 2)

**green**
(page 3)

**blue**
(page 2)

**fire**
(page 3)

**red**
(page 2)

**war dance**
(page 4)

23

play
(page 5)

leaf
(page 11)

traffic
lights
(page 7)

lion
(page 12)

berries
(page 8)

grass
(page 12)

bird
(page 8)

chameleon
(page 13)

insect
(page 10)

foot-
ballers
(page 16)

flag
(page 17)

ink
(page 19)

dye
(page 18)

rainbow
(page 21)

book
(page 19)

rain
(page 21)

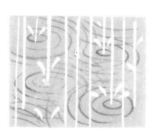

dot
(page 19)

cork
(page 22)